See Oh See How I Love Thee?

A READ-TOGETHER BOOK

by the Sisters of Children of Mary

This book is small but a mighty help in learning the essentials of the Catholic faith and in getting to know Jesus better and loving Him more—and the more you love Him, the happier you will be!

In accord with the *Code of Canon Law,* I hereby grant the *Imprimatur* ("Permission to Publish") regarding the manuscript entitled *See Oh See How I Love Thee?*

Imprimatur: ✝   Most Reverend Joseph R. Binzer
Auxiliary Bishop
Archdiocese of Cincinnati
November 21, 2019

love for Love Publishing

5440 Moeller Ave
Cincinnati, OH 45212
childrenofmary.net

*Dedicated to the Torchbearers of the Queen
and their families*

*"I need you, my children, to be Torchbearers
of Divine Love"*

~Our Lady of America

Did you know that there was a time when nothing existed except God? There was no grass... no sky... no earth... no color... no time... no planets... no stars... no universe... no animals... no people... nothing...

There was ONLY GOD!

Who is God?
What is God like?
Some of His attributes are:

—**He is Eternal:** He has no beginning and
no end

—**He is All-powerful**
    He created everything out of nothing.

—**He knows everything**

even your
thoughts
and your
feelings.

God is Love
and
HE LOVES YOU
more than anyone can.
And what does He want from you?
LOVE!

Why did
God create
you?

To know Him,
love Him,
and
serve Him
in this life
and to be
happy
with Him
forever
in Heaven.

When you love Him, you become like Him,
and you are united—together as one!

In fact, He loves you so much
that He became man for two reasons:

1. To redeem you

He died on the Cross and opened
the gates of Heaven.

So now you can be baptized and become a child
of God and receive God's life into your soul. As
a child of God, you can get to Heaven by loving
and obeying Him so that you can always be
united with Him in this life and in the next.

2. To remain on earth with us in the Holy Eucharist

so you could love Him,
and He could shower you with
the graces you need to get to Heaven.

How do you get to Heaven?
You get to Heaven by loving God with all your
heart, especially loving Jesus in the
Most Holy Eucharist, because
the Holy Eucharist is God with us!

Jesus is true God and true man, but only one
person—the Second Person of the Blessed
Trinity. Jesus is God. He stays with us in the
Holy Eucharist, thirsting for our love!

We receive special
graces from adoring
Jesus in the Most
Blessed Sacrament!
We grow to love Him
more and feel a very

special, deep closeness with Jesus, and a grow-
ing awareness of His presence in our midst.

Jesus wants you to receive Him with love in Holy Communion.

When we receive Jesus with love in Holy Communion, we are united with Him more than at any other time on earth!

We receive special graces from receiving Jesus in Holy Communion: to love God above all things and to love others as Jesus loves them.

Pope Pius X said that, if the angels were capable of envy, they would envy us for being able to receive Jesus in Holy Communion.

JESUS, I LOVE YOU
IN THE MOST BLESSED SACRAMENT

Do you see the little girl receiving Jesus on the tongue? Some people receive Our Lord in the hand, and that is permitted in some places. But it is the law of the Church to receive Communion on the tongue, and that is the most reverent way. We encourage everyone to receive Him in this most reverent way, and say to Him as you receive Him, "Jesus, I love You! Jesus, I love You!" This makes Jesus very happy, and brings much grace to the whole world. Tell Him you love Him over and over all day long!

We tell Jesus we love Him with our words and with our actions. In fact, actions speak louder than words! To remain united with God in love, we must obey the Ten Commandments and the Church teachings. The first and most important thing we must do is go to Holy Mass every Sunday and on Holy Days of Obligation:

January 1, the Solemnity of Mary, Mother of God

Thursday of the Sixth Week of Easter, the Solemnity of the Ascension

August 15, the Solemnity of the Assumption of the Blessed Virgin Mary

November 1, the Solemnity of All Saints

December 8, the Solemnity of the Immaculate Conception

December 25, the Solemnity of the Nativity of Our Lord Jesus Christ

 The Mass is the perfect prayer because it is Jesus offering His life to God the Father. It is a great miracle! When I go to Mass, I am not just remembering Jesus or thinking about what He did a long time ago. NO! It is like getting into a time machine and actually being at the Cross with Mother Mary, as Jesus hangs crucified on the Cross. At Mass, we love Him and offer our lives to God the Father, along with Jesus' offering.

We receive special graces at Mass—to love
God and surrender our whole lives to Him.

Many people go to Mass every day; those who are able to do so are very wise, but we *must* go at least on Sundays and Holy Days of Obligation. It is a grave offense against God to miss Mass on those days. That is how important Holy Mass is! It is the most important thing that happens on earth every day! Each Mass has the same value as Jesus' crucifixion!

He died for us; we don't want to wound His Heart by not going to Mass on Sunday. What a joy it is for Jesus when we go willingly to Holy Mass and receive Him with love! Then He can become your best friend and help you find peace and joy in this life and forever in Heaven.

Loving Jesus brings joy.

A Catholic cannot help but be happy

"I suffered a lot but my soul was singing."

because God dwells in our Church!

In every Catholic Church you are in the presence of the King!

If you were in the presence of a king, you would not talk loudly or run, but would walk slowly, and approach him respectfully.

If you wanted to be friends with a king, you would greet him joyfully and give him all your attention.

Jesus is the King of Kings. When you are at Mass, pray like the the little boy in this picture and follow all that is happening at the altar. This will honor Jesus very much and show Him you really love Him.

It is great to be Catholic!

"Catholic" means universal. God wants everyone to be Catholic, because Jesus established only one Church—the Holy Roman Catholic Church. He gave priests in His Church the power to forgive sins so that, when we receive Holy Communion, we will be filled with His grace and worthy to receive Him. He also gave priests the power to change bread and wine into His Body and Blood—that is called transubstantiation. At Mass, when the priest says the words, "This is My Body... This is My Blood," the bread and wine become Jesus, the living Jesus, Who is God! In Holy Communion we receive a living Person; we receive God! This is called the Holy Eucharist or the Most Blessed Sacrament.

"Jesus, I love You in the Most Blessed Sacrament!"

Jesus wants all of us to be saints; but, while on earth, all of us do bad things; only in Heaven will we be perfect. In Heaven everyone will be filled with love and joy and peace. Here on earth, we sinners must do our best and pray for one another, go to Confession frequently, receive Jesus with love in Holy Communion as often as we can, and be kind and loving toward one another.

We need Jesus to be good. That is why he gives us the Holy Catholic Church—so we can go to Confession and receive Him with love in Holy Communion.

I will never stop being Catholic!

It is there I find truth.

The Catholic Church is the One True Church.

God Became Man and Established Only One Church

33 A.D. Jesus Christ Founded The Catholic Church

All Christians were united—
one Church, one Faith, one Lord—until...

Since God established
His Church, many—mere men—
broke away from that Church, leading millions astray.

The fruit of this rejection of truth and embracing
relativism is division: thousands of denominations
each professing its own leader's personal interpretations.

Let's pray that all Christians will unite so they too
may enjoy the great gifts God has given His Church.

Catholic means "Universal"—It's for everyone!

It's great to be Catholic!

*"Father, that they may be one, even as We are one,
that the world may believe that You sent Me..." Jn 17*

1054 Greek Orthodox

1517

1534 Anglican

Protestant Denominations

1517 Lutherans
1521 Anabaptists
1534 Anglicans
1536 Calvinists
1560 Presbyterians
1609 Baptists
1739 Methodists
1789 Episcopal
1830 Mormons
1874 Jehovah's Witnesses

AND

THOUSANDS of other
Protestant Denominations

Jesusreignoverus@gmail.com

15

Appendix

How do we know where to find the true Church?
Apostolic Succession

The early Christians had no doubts about how to determine which was the true Church and which doctrines the true teachings of Christ. The test was simple: just trace the apostolic succession of the claimants. Apostolic succession is the line of bishops stretching back to the apostles. All over the world, all Catholic bishops are part of a lineage that goes back to the time of the apostles, something that is impossible in Protestant denominations (most of which do not even claim to have bishops).

The role of apostolic succession in preserving true doctrine is illustrated in the Bible. To make sure that the apostles' teachings would be passed down after the deaths of the apostles, Paul told Timothy, "What you have heard from me before many witnesses entrust to faithful men who will be able to teach others also." (2 Tim. 2:2). In this passage he refers to the first three generations of apostolic succession—his own generation, Timothy's generation, and the generation Timothy will teach. The Church Fathers, who were links in that chain of succession, regularly appealed to apostolic succession as a test for whether Catholics or heretics had correct doctrine.*

  *https://www.catholic.com/tract/apostolic-succession

How We Receive Reflects What We Believe

An often repeated story:

A man took a non-Catholic to Mass with him one Sunday. After the Mass, the non-Catholic said, "You told me you believe that what you receive in Holy Communion is really God. When I saw everyone going up to receive, they were not acting like that was God; they were receiving Him like popcorn. And after Mass, everyone was just talking and laughing like nothing special had happened. If I believed what you believe, I would have crawled up on my knees weeping to receive my God."

Actions Speak Louder Than Words

For hundreds of years, all Catholic churches all over the world had a communion rail, and everyone knelt at the rail and received Jesus in Holy Communion on the tongue; it was the law of the Church. Now the Church allows Communion in the hand; an indult (an exception to the law) was granted to the U.S. in 1969, but the law of the Church to receive Jesus in Holy Communion on the tongue remains.

Cardinal Sarah, Prefect of the Congregation for Divine Worship, encourages everyone to follow the law of the Church and receive Holy Communion on the tongue and kneeling:

"The greatness and nobility of man, as well as the highest expression of his love for his creator, consists in kneeling before God. Let

us come as children and humbly receive the Body of Christ on our knees and on our tongue... Mother Teresa of Calcutta was saddened and pained when she saw Christians receiving Holy Communion in their hand."

The Family That Prays Together Stays Together!

It is of vital importance that Our Lord be the center of our family life through daily family prayer. When children grow up witnessing the love and devotion of their parents and seeing that they encourage them in the same love and devotion, they then have a firm foundation that will enable them to grow to the fullest potential of holiness God has destined for them. When we neglect prayer as a family, we witness by our actions that something is more important than our relationship with God. The devil may try to mess with our priorities; we must be strong in our convictions and not allow anything but our True King to rule our lives.

Enthrone Jesus in Your Home

A young man witnessed the love and devotion of his parents who had enthroned their home to the Sacred Heart of Jesus. Each night they all gathered around the image of Our Lord and prayed a prayer consecrating their whole family to His Heart. This inspired him to love the living Sacred Heart of Jesus in the Eucharist. In May 2019, this young man was ordained a priest for the Archdiocese of Cincinnati.

We encourage all families, if you have not already, to enthrone the Sacred Heart of Jesus in your home—making a sacred space to gather and pray, a grace-filled domestic church!

"There is no problem, I tell you, no matter how difficult it is, that we cannot resolve by the prayer of the Holy Rosary."

Our Lady of Fatima

"The Most Holy Virgin, in these last times in which we live, has given a new efficacy to the recitation of the Rosary to such an extent that there is no problem—no matter how difficult it is—whether temporal or above all spiritual, in the personal life of each one of us and of our families…that cannot be solved by the Rosary." (Sister Lucia dos Santos, Fatima seer)

"Certain fashions will be introduced that will offend Our Lord very much."
Our Lady of Fatima, 1917

How beautiful to be lady-like,

like Our Lady.

A Catholic Man
Being a great leader, provider, and protector is every man's mission

As spiritual heads of the family, fathers lead their families

—Leader: by their example of faithfulness to Jesus and His Church by their strong prayer life and their witness of virtue

—Provider: providing both spiritual and temporal needs

—Protector: protecting their wives and daughters with high standards of modesty and behavior

The father has the privilege and the duty to guide his son into manhood.

Union with God
Living in the State of Grace

To benefit from receiving Jesus in Holy Communion, we must be in the state of grace; that is, if we have committed serious sin, we must go to Confession before receiving Him. To receive Jesus in Holy Communion not in the state of grace is to commit another serious sin; it is a sacrilege.

A serious, grave or mortal sin is the knowing and willful violation of God's law in a serious matter, for example, idolatry, adultery, murder, slander, and missing Holy Mass on Sundays and Holy Days of Obligation. These are all things gravely contrary to the love we owe God and, because of Him, our neighbor. As Jesus taught, when condemning even looking at a woman lustfully, sin can be both interior (choices of the will alone) or exterior (choices of the will carried into action). A man who willfully desires to fornicate, steal, murder or commit some other grave sin, has already seriously offended God by choosing interiorly what God has prohibited. Mortal sin is called mortal because it is the "spiritual" death of the soul (separation from God). So, if we die without repenting in this state of mortal sin, the soul cannot enter Heaven and will spend all eternity in Hell. However, by turning our hearts back to Him and receiving the Sacrament of Penance, we are restored to His friendship. Catholics are not allowed to receive Communion if they have unconfessed mortal sins.

For mortal sin, it must not only be 1) serious matter, 2) the person must know it is serious and then 3) freely commit it.

Venial sins are offensive to God, but they do not break our friendship with God, although they injure it.

For example, imagine there is a vase in a museum worth five million dollars. A person comes along with a nail and scratches the vase, greatly diminishing its value. Another person comes along, picks up the vase, throws it on the gound and shatters it into numberless, tiny pieces, making it good for nothing. A venial sin would be comparable to a scratch; a mortal sin like the shattered vase.

The great news is that God, knowing our weakness, gave us the great gift of Confession, where—with deep contrition, humbly confessing our sins—God takes the shattered pieces of our lives and remakes us in His own image, even more beautiful than before!

Kings 5: 14 Naaman was a captain to a great king of Aram. With his flesh, putrid and rotting with leprosy, he went to the prophet Elisha in Samaria to be cured. "So he went down and dipped himself in the Jordan seven times, as the man of God had told him, and his flesh was restored and became clean like that of a young boy."

Examination of Conscience for Teens

FIRST COMMANDMENT
I am the Lord your God. You shall not have strange gods before me.

☐ Do I really love God above all things or have I made other things—money, clothes, sports, TV, music, pleasure, peer approval—more important than God?

☐ Do I give time every day to God in prayer? Do I pray only when I need something or do I also seek to praise and thank God, too?

☐ Do I put my trust in superstitions, good luck charms, rather than God alone?

☐ Do I make a serious effort to get to know my faith well, since my relationship with God is supposed to be the most important thing in my life?

☐ Have I rejected any Church teaching or denied that I was a Catholic? Do I pick and choose only the parts of God's message that please me?

SECOND COMMANDMENT
You shall not take the name of the Lord your God in vain.

☐ Have I used the words "God" or "Jesus" carelessly, in anger or when surprised?

☐ Have I used foul or ugly language? Have I wished evil on another?

☐ Have I shown disrespect for the Blessed Virgin Mary, the saints, the Church and those who have consecrated their lives to God?

THIRD COMMANDMENT
Remember to keep holy the Lord's Day.

☐ Have I missed Mass on Sunday or any holy day of obligation through my own fault?

☐ Do I arrive at church late or leave early due to

carelessness or without serious reason?

- ☐ Am I reverent and pay attention during Mass?
- ☐ Do I avoid unnecessary work on Sunday? Do I make Sunday just another part of the weekend or do I use it for acts of love toward God, my family and those in need?

FOURTH COMMANDMENT
Honor your father and your mother.

- ☐ Do I try to bring happiness and peace to my family or do I cause tension and division?
- ☐ Do I respect and obey my parents?
- ☐ Have I dishonored or mistreated my parents or members of my family by word or deed?
- ☐ Am I willing to help around the house or must I be nagged a hundred times?
- ☐ Do I try to get along with my brothers and sisters or am I a bully to my siblings?
- ☐ Do I give a good example, especially to younger siblings?
- ☐ Do I respect others in authority: priests, nuns, police, my elders?
- ☐ Do I make time to visit my elderly relatives?

FIFTH COMMANDMENT
You shall not kill.

- ☐ Have I been violent toward others in word or action?
- ☐ Do I intentionally cut or harm my own body, forgetting that it is a Temple of God?
- ☐ Do I say cruel things, or make fun of others intending to hurt their feelings? Do I say cruel things about others behind their backs?
- ☐ Have I stopped speaking to anyone? Do I hold any grudges or try to get even with others? Have I failed to forgive others?
- ☐ Do I get angry easily or lose my temper?

28

SIXTH COMMANDMENT
You shall not commit adultery.

- ☐ Do I treat my body and other people's bodies with purity and respect?
- ☐ Do I look at television shows, movies, or pictures that do not respect the human body?
- ☐ Am I modest in my speech and the clothes I wear?
- ☐ Do I talk to others about sex or our bodies in a way that does not respect God's gift of sexuality?
- ☐ Do I treat others, in my deeds or thoughts, as objects?
- ☐ Have I failed to remain chaste in mind and body within my relationship with my boyfriend/girlfriend?

SEVENTH COMMANDMENT
You shall not steal.

- ☐ Have I been greedy or jealous of things others have? Do I resent their popularity or success?
- ☐ Have I taken things that were not mine from a store or another person?
- ☐ Have I destroyed or misused another person's property for fun, or by accident without owning up to it?
- ☐ Do i return things that I borrow? In good condition?
- ☐ Have I wasted time, goods or food?
- ☐ Do I generously share what I have with those in need?

EIGHTH COMMANDMENT
You shall not commit false witness against your neighbor.

- ☐ Have I kept my promises?
- ☐ Did I break a secret or a confidence?
- ☐ Am I honest in my school work?
- ☐ Do I tell lies to make myself look good?
- ☐ Do I tell lies to protect myself from punishment?
- ☐ Do I tell lies that make another person look bad or get them in trouble?

NINTH COMMANDMENT
You shall not covet your neighbor's wife.

- ☐ Do I allow my parents to spend time with one another, or do I get jealous and want them to pay attention only to me?
- ☐ Do I get mad when I have to share my friends?
- ☐ Are there kids I will not be friends with or am mean to because they look different?

TENTH COMMANDMENT
You shall not covet your neighbor's goods.

- ☐ Am I jealous or envious of the things or abilities that others have?
- ☐ Am I thankful to God and my parents for what they have given me?
- ☐ Do I share the things I have with my family, friends and with the poor?

Act of Contrition:

O my God, I am heartily sorry for having offended You, and I detest all my sins, because of Your just punishments, but most of all because they offend You, my God, Who are all-good and deserving of all my love. I firmly intend, with your help, to sin no more and to avoid whatever leads me to sin.

Examination of Conscience for Children

1. **I am the Lord your God. You shall not have strange gods before me.**
    - ☐ Have I wanted more things, making things or money more important than God?
    - ☐ Have I made an idol of sports or entertainment figures?

2. **You shall not take the name of the Lord your God in vain.**
    - ☐ Do I use God's name carelessly?
    - ☐ Do I use God's name in anger?

3. **Remember to keep holy the Lord's Day.**
    - ☐ Did I attend Mass on Sunday?
    - ☐ Did my behavior make it difficult or impossible for my parents to get to church on time?
    - ☐ Have I remembered to pray daily?

4. **Honor your father and your mother.**
    - ☐ Do I obey my parents?
    - ☐ Have I done my chores without complaining?
    - ☐ Do I do my chores without being reminded?
    - ☐ Have I been disrespectful to teachers, coaches or others in authority?

5. **You shall not kill.**
    - ☐ Do I keep my patience or do I lose my temper?
    - ☐ Do I hold grudges and try to get even with others?
    - ☐ Have I been unfair to others, especially those who are different than I am?

6.   You shall not commit adultery.
- ☐ Do I show respect for my body?
- ☐ Do I respect the bodies of others?
- ☐ Do I avoid harmful things like drugs, tobacco and alcohol?

7.   You shall not steal.
- ☐ Have I taken something that belongs to someone else?
- ☐ Have I "forgotten" to return something that I borrowed?
- ☐ Have I used money responsibly?

8.   You shall not bear false witness against your neighbor.
- ☐ Do I play fairly or do I ever cheat at school or games?
- ☐ Have I been honest or have I lied?
- ☐ Have I hurt someone by what I have said or done?
- ☐ Have I copied someone else's homework?

9.   You shall not covet your neighbor's wife.
- ☐ Have I been jealous of the friends that someone else has?
- ☐ Have I tried to be kind to others?

10.   You shall not covet your neighbor's goods.
- ☐ Have I been jealous of the things that my friends have?
- ☐ Have I nagged my parents into buying things because my friends have them?
- ☐ Have I helped others when they needed help?

We hope you will say the prayer below. Our ardent desire is that Jesus will be enthroned in every heart, in every home, and on every altar, and soon, please Lord, proclaimed King of America. To see the video and learn more, visit our website loveforlove.net.

Jesus, Reign Over Us

Make America Holy

WE LOVE YOU, JESUS! REIGN OVER US!

Enthroning Jesus in My Heart

Most merciful Jesus, I come and kneel before You Who are truly alive and present on this altar. With every fiber of my being, I make an act of faith in Your words, "I AM the living bread come down from Heaven." Yes, my Lord, I believe it because You have said it, and I am ready to give my life to maintain this truth!

I wish to enthrone You in my heart as King and Ruler over my whole life. Therefore, I make a spiritual communion right now and invite You into my heart to take complete possession of it.

33

Rule and reign over me, my God--every area of my life, especially in those areas in which I find it most difficult to submit myself to Your Most Holy Will.

I formally and solemnly proclaim and enthrone You, Jesus Eucharistic, as King of my heart. I completely surrender to You my family, my vocation, my loved ones, my social life, my work, my leisure, my eating, my sleeping and every aspect of my life.

I now formally dethrone myself from the throne of my heart, and call to mind and bring to You my predominant sins and faults, casting down the idol of my selfishness so that You may reign gloriously in me. I will obey Your commandments and embrace all that Your Holy Catholic Church teaches. That this offering and enthronement may not be mere lip service or a mockery, and that I may have sufficient grace to unite my will to Your will in all things, I promise and commit to receive You in Holy Communion with great love, telling You over and over again, "I love You. I love You with all my heart." I want to quench Your thirst to be loved in the Most Blessed Sacrament.

Yes, Jesus, I belong to You entirely and forever. I am eternally grateful for Your unfathomable mercy which has led You to never leave me; You are all mine in this Sacrament of Love.